SIGN *with* *your* BABY™

How to Communicate with Infants Before They Can Speak

Joseph Garcia

Co-Published by

Northlight Communications
A division of Northlight, LLC
11395 Fifth Avenue Northeast
Seattle, WA 98125-6108

Stratton-Kehl Publications, Inc.
P.O. Box 28567
Bellingham, WA 98228-0567

More information about *Sign with your Baby* products can be found in the back of this book.

Library of Congress Catalog Card Number 98-89288
ISBN 0-9636229-2-7

Cover Design
Graphica
Communication
Solutions

Illustrations
Gregory Maes
Heather Nystrom
Lola Roberson
Joseph Garcia

Cartoons
Matt Anderson

Layout
Terry Stratton
Dara Burrows
Joseph Garcia
Stephanie Hopkinson

Proof Reading
Barbara J. Miller

I want to give special thanks to Dara Burrows, my wife, for her patience and persistence in transforming my thesis into a readable guide. I also thank John Herum for his technical guidance.

I am grateful to the early childhood development researchers whose studies continue to help us become better parents. And a special acknowledgment goes to Dr. Glenn Massay who encouraged me to investigate my idea, test my theories, and write this book.

Printed on recycled paper with soy ink.

For my parents, Emma and Bill Garcia,
who taught me that through learning
and loving, I could do anything.

FOREWORD

Certain very important facts about human language have been known for many years. Two thirds to three quarters of all everyday language is ordinarily acquired by the third birthday. Also, in cases of poor educational performance, inadequate language ability is almost invariably present. What has not been known, surprisingly, is what exactly goes on during those first three years that underlies the acquisition of language. The reason for this strange state of affairs is that the research community has largely neglected the details of development during these early years. Recently, however, important progress has been made.

Even some thirty years ago reports appeared that indicated that children taught sign language had acquired about seventy-five signs by the time they were nine months old. In contrast, the typical child of that age could understand fewer than ten words, regardless of how bright she was.

This was a tantalizing though isolated finding. Until fairly recently, no one in developmental research followed up on this potentially important finding. Now two programs have. One of them is the subject of this book.

I recommend the teaching of signs, starting at about seven months of age, for several reasons. First, sign language represents a second language, and our research consistently showed that when a second language was introduced in an effective manner to a child from the early months on, the child would not only become bilingual by the second birthday, but would be ahead of the monolingual child in both languages! Indeed, that has been the experience of parents in our program.

Second, we have repeatedly found that children, especially boys, though developing well, have few or no spoken words at all until their second birthdays. We have also learned that the period between seventeen and twenty months of age is a particularly difficult time, in that the normal child is very limited in regard to frustration tolerance, and being unable to express himself exacerbates the problem. A child who can sign at that stage of life is a child who will cause considerably less frustration for himself and his parents. That means the attachment process can move along much more smoothly and probably to a better outcome.

Finally, the potential for understanding mental activity in children between eight and twenty-two months of age that is made possible by sign language is intriguing. Someday soon we will take advantage of this remarkable tool to get a much more refined picture of how the mind of a child evolves.

For all these reasons, and because his work is sound, I strongly recommend this groundbreaking work of Joseph Garcia.

Burton L. White, Ph.D., June 1998
Director, The Center for Parent Education
Author, *The First Three Years of Life* and
Raising a Happy Unspoiled Child

CONTENTS

Communication: The Backbone to a Healthy
    Relationship With Your Child 9

911...To Call or Not to Call? 11

Proving an Intuition 13

Get the Big Picture 15

Something Done Wrong Long Enough Becomes Right? 15

Why the First Signs of Intelligent Life Can Be Signs 17

"Even Though I Can't Talk Yet, I Know More Than
    You Think I Know" 19

How Your Child's Cognitive Skills and Motor
    Coordination Develop During Infancy 20

Seeing the World Through a Newcomer's Eyes 21

Shared Perception and Shared Meaning 21

Learning by Association 23

Will Signing Interfere With My
    Child's Speech Development? 24

To Contribute or to Commit? 25

How to Sign With Your Baby.. 26

Let Your Fingers Do the Talking 26

Gazes: Opportune Moments to Introduce Signs 26

Let's Face It 28

The First Signs of Intelligent Life 29

How To Show Your Infant a Sign 29

Which Signs to Start With and When to Start 31

"Can You Tell Me Where It Hurts?" 39

Some Handy Games 41

Recognizing Your Children's Signs 43

Repeating and Reinforcing Your Signs 46

Combining Signs 48

How to Create a New Sign 48

The Power of Silence 49

Things to Remember 50

The Terrible Twos and Threes:
        Talk Your Child Out of Them 51

Final Thoughts 52

Hand Shapes 55

Vocabulary 57

References 107

Index 108

COMMUNICATION: THE BACKBONE TO A HEALTHY RELATIONSHIP WITH YOUR CHILD

From the moment babies are born, these tiny human beings start communicating with the world around them. The vital connection between you and your infants depends on this communication. Infants will use extensive body language, facial expressions, and all sorts of verbal sounds to interact with you. These movements and sounds will eventually evolve into language. But until they do, you may have an incredibly difficult time understanding your infants' attempts to tell you things.

How many times have you wished you could look into your babies' minds and know what was going on in there? How many parents have felt the instinctual longing to extract a thought or a word from their troubled infants? The inability to understand your infants is certainly not because you don't try hard enough, nor is it because the infants abandon their attempts to express themselves. Infants have an instinctual need to communicate with you, just as you have an instinctual need to understand them.

Infants are born with abundant intelligence. However, they have a limited means to let you know what their thoughts and needs are. Their undeveloped vocal cords restrict them from participating in the verbal language around them. Imagine how it must feel to be a baby who has many specific needs and thoughts to express, but has no effective way to make those specific needs or thoughts understood. At times, it must be frustrating for these small and socially dependent beings to live with these limitations.

Communication is one of the highest forms of social interaction. Leading researchers in infant behavior have determined that social interaction is crucial to all infants' development. They have further concluded that for a caregiver to withhold social responses to an infant's attempts to communicate is one of the most disruptive things that can occur in the infant's learning process.

What can you do to *encourage* this learning process? Here is where *Sign with your Baby* can contribute to your infants' development. Imagine how your babies might feel if one day you started using simple hand movements to communicate. Let's say you make a particular motion during a certain daily activity, such as eating. Soon your infants associate that movement with the situation or activity that was taking place when the motion was introduced. They begin to experiment with their own hands and discover they can replicate the movements you make. Receiving reinforcement from you, babies quickly learn that by making this motion, they can communicate their needs and wants.

The time between birth and when your infants utter their first recognizable words can be a time of miscommunication or a time when your communication is less than precise. This does not have to be the case. These precious months can be rich in meaningful and effective infant/parent interaction. Using manual communication with your infants can help build a solid foundation for mutual understanding, dramatically contributing to the bonding process.

911... TO CALL OR NOT TO CALL?

As a parent, I found that there was nothing more frightening, frustrating, or heartbreaking than when my young toddler came to me crying and I had no idea what was wrong. I can remember being a toddler and not understanding why the rest of the world didn't know what I was feeling. It never dawned on me that it would take more than crying to let my parents know what was wrong.

The somewhat unusual anecdote that follows illustrates, first of all, that strange and scary things really can happen to your toddler. It also shows one extremely practical reason for learning some simple signs.

Imagine your toddler Juliet is eleven months old and just learning to walk. She hasn't made her first solo step, but she can really cover some ground balancing herself against the couch. She is doing just that when she plops down onto her bottom, rolls over on her tummy, and happily explores the floor underneath the couch.

She laughs and coos and makes her delightful infant noises. She's been exploring her vocal chords lately, and has come up with some wild sounds. But she hasn't said any clear words yet, other than "mama," "papa," "bye bye" and "uh oh."

Suddenly her bubbling banter turns to a distressed whimper. She sits up and turns to find you. You are sitting nearby wondering what happened. Then Juliet looks at you intently and stops her crying for a moment while she raises her hands and bumps the tips of her index fingers together in front of her nose.

You recognize her hand motion—it means pain. You've been showing her this sign for about three months. After watching you do it, now she can make the sign. And, not only does she know what the sign means, but she can use it to tell you about her pain.

You pick Juliet up, thinking to yourself, "She made the gesture in front of her nose, so that's where she must hurt." You examine her nose. "Hmmm…it looks okay, but she's still crying. Maybe she bumped her nose on the floor."

Then she looks at you and repeats her sign in front of her nose. You wonder, "What can be wrong?" You bend her head back slightly and look a little closer. That's when you see something lodged way up inside her nostril. It's her brother's toy train wheel that broke off his train that morning.

You carefully remove the wheel from Juliet's nose, and soon her crying stops. She looks at you with satisfaction. She was able to tell you what was wrong. You were able to respond. What a relief!

PROVING AN INTUITION

I've always been intrigued by manual language, even though no one in my family is deaf. So, in 1975, I learned American Sign Language. I enjoyed signing and soon began using it in my work and social life. I was spending time with my deaf friends, some of whom had hearing children. I noticed that hearing children of deaf parents started communicating with sign language at an earlier age than other hearing children did with words.

Intrigued by this observation, I decided to research early childhood language acquisition and the part sign language could play in this process. In 1986, I was in graduate school and chose this topic for my thesis. I read about the research that had already been done in pre-speech communication and became especially inspired by the work of Margaret Bullowa, Katherine Nelson, and Timothy Moore. These researchers confirmed that pre-speech infants have the intelligence to communicate specific thoughts and needs.

As I researched further, I found plenty of information on deaf children and their language development. But I couldn't find much information on hearing children using sign language (such as siblings of deaf children using signs). I wondered, what would be the result of using signs for early communication between hearing children and hearing parents. The more I researched, the more I became convinced that I was uncovering a treasure!

My next step was to find out how much earlier a child could communicate with signs than with words. After consulting with experts in infant development and conducting field research, I concluded that you can begin parent/infant communication at eight months using signs, rather than waiting for comprehensible speech to develop at sixteen to eighteen months.

The births of my two sons in 1985 and 1987 gave me perfect opportunities to develop and use the method of teaching signs to babies. Looking into my new-born sons' eyes, I could see and feel their innate intelligence and their desire to communicate. It was exciting to be living out, in my day-to-day interactions, the theories and ideas I had been researching. It's hard for me to put into words how wonderful I felt when my sons began to communicate with me at such an early age. Our communication helped me become more in tune, not only with my children, but also with myself as a parent.

Many other parents have also experienced these rewards. Parents participating in my studies included parents with no signing experience and some with limited signing experience. All the parents were surprised at how young their infants were when they started signing. They were also extremely grateful for this tool. Since the printing of my book, *Toddler Talk*, thousands of families have successfully learned how to sign with their babies.

GET THE BIG PICTURE

To get the big picture, please read the entire book before you try anything with your infants. It's important that you understand what's involved in infant communication before you start introducing signs. There's a little bit of background and discussion followed by how-to steps and suggestions. The vocabulary section at the end of the book has drawings and instructions explaining each sign. You can use the vocabulary section as a workbook and keep track of your child's progress, or write notes and reminders to yourself.

SOMETHING DONE WRONG LONG ENOUGH BECOMES RIGHT?

Believe it or not, in the 1930s many pediatricians in this country told parents that infants were too fragile to be picked up or cuddled. People actually viewed holding and touching infants as something harmful. Most parents followed this advice. Finally, in the 1940s, a publication refuting this view went around the country and this attitude began to change. Not until then were parents advised that it was okay to pick up and play with their infants.

Although it may be difficult to imagine that so recently in our history infants were seldom cuddled or caressed, this was the norm. Similarly, for years people have seen manual communication only as a tool for the Deaf. I've encountered people with the attitude that a person who signs is defective or somehow less than normal—whatever "normal" means. Fortunately, we are constantly discovering and adopting more sensible ways to approach new and different things.

Communication, like physical contact, is an essential component in our children's development. We can benefit from the powerful gift the Deaf have given us. That gift is actually a treasure waiting to be unlocked. And the key to that treasure is in your hands.

WHY THE FIRST SIGNS OF INTELLIGENT LIFE CAN BE SIGNS

Most people haven't used sign language, so it may be hard to imagine communicating without spoken words. This is why many parents wait until their child can clearly speak before they earnestly begin to focus on two-way communication. However, recent studies indicate that children can absorb and communicate information shortly after birth.

Authorities suggest that 90% of the information we absorb is received through our vision. This means visual acuity is extremely important in our overall development. Infants will naturally use vision to help guide them through the early months of life.

Infants naturally use smiling, cooing, and crying to communicate their needs and feelings. They understand a lot about themselves and the world around them. What they lack is a precise way to express themselves, such as "Mommy, my stomach hurts" or "I want more food."

Infants are naturally attracted by movement, especially when the movement is made by mama, papa, or other caregivers. When you sign, your baby will observe your visual communication patterns and eventually relate your motions to meanings.

Most infants' vocal cords must develop for sixteen or more months before they can pronounce clear words. Usually, children don't begin speaking in two- and three-word sentences until they are eighteen to twenty-one months old.

However, visual and muscular coordination are in place much earlier than that—long before vocal skills mature. In other words, your infants have the ability to use their hands to make signs before they can use speech to clearly communicate. Through signing, you will give your infants a way to express themselves that will be more precise and effective than smiling, cooing, and crying. Your young toddlers can use single signs (and many times several signs together) nearly one year before they effectively use speech.

Signs themselves have certain advantages over words. Signs are often iconic—they represent the shape of objects or mimic an activity or movement. Therefore, they can be easily recognized and remembered. Words, on the other hand (no pun intended), are more arbitrary and lack an obvious connection to what is being expressed.

Take the sign **EAT**, for example. The hand mimics putting something in the mouth. The word "eat" could be said in a number of different languages and sound different in each. But what other gesture, anywhere on the earth, could better show the action of eating?

EAT

"EVEN THOUGH I CAN'T TALK YET, I KNOW MORE THAN YOU THINK I KNOW"

Your infants are born intelligent and have quite a sophisticated idea of what is going on much earlier than many people may think. This intelligence needs to be nurtured by you, the caregiver. The learning process begins moments after birth and quickly accelerates during the first few months of life. Infants are born with a hunger for your contact and communication. They are continuously searching for ways to express themselves. They are looking to you for cues to help them communicate their needs and express their feelings.

Infants can make sense of our complex world long before they can react to it through signs or speech. Your infants understand that communication is going on. They want to be part of that communication much earlier than they are able to tell you. In their desire to express themselves, they will use whatever mode of communication is presented to them.

HOW YOUR CHILD'S COGNITIVE SKILLS AND MOTOR COORDINATION DEVELOP DURING INFANCY

Dr. Eugene Johnson, a child psychologist, has provided the following overview of a typical child's mental and physical development during the first two years of life. He divided infant development into stages—4 months, 8 months, 12 months, etc. These stages are averages based on the many infants observed in research. However, remember that all infants are unique, and will have their own individual timetables. According to Dr. Johnson:

> Growth during the first two years is more rapid than at any other time in one's life. Research suggests that, by the age of 4 months, infants are capable of remembering sounds and objects, as well as examining parts of their bodies. At 8 months they can play some social games and begin to imitate gestures and actions performed by adults. At this stage they are potentially ready for learning signs. Their motor skills have developed to a point where they are capable of manipulating objects in their hands and standing with support.

> By 12 months, infants begin to pretend by symbolically representing familiar activities, such as drinking and eating. They begin to develop choice and will select activities that are desirable. Motor development has continued to improve and further abilities to produce signs have increased. A better understanding of the use of objects and their intended purposes has developed. Advanced motor skills support the development of an increasing number of signs.

> By the end of infancy, at 24 months, cognitive development has improved to a point where children are consistently representing objects with

verbal responses and possibly with signs. Motor coordination has developed to a point where more fluid movements are possible, allowing for a larger sign vocabulary.

SEEING THE WORLD THROUGH A NEWCOMER'S EYES

In their first few months of life, much of what infants experience is new. Infants do not perceive the world from an adult's perspective because infants have fewer memories or associations from which to draw. Thinking is nothing more than combining and rearranging what is in our memory. The more memories we have, the more raw material we possess to support our thoughts.

Often, infants are experiencing things for the first time that you've seen countless times. These experiences can make profound impressions on infants' minds and help form the basis for their learning.

Conversations with my parents reveal that some things I clearly recall from my early years totally escaped them. Apparently, those things stuck in my memory, but were insignificant to my parents. The idea is that you never know what event will fix itself in your infant's memory. Be sensitive to your infant's perception. Your increased sensitivity will help you understand the potential impact anything can have on your infant's memories.

SHARED PERCEPTION AND SHARED MEANING

You need to be alert to your children's perception; it is their perception that will determine the meaning they associate with the signs you show them. Your ability to connect with them on their level of perception will help them learn how to communicate.

Infants will give the meaning you intend to a sign if it is shown to them in the correct situation—at a moment when both of you are experiencing the same thing. They will automatically connect that sign to the shared experience. Therefore, you establish shared meaning between you and your infants through the signs you give to them.

Imagine you are looking at a beautiful sunset and you hold your toddler Joey up to see it too. Then, you show him the sign that means sunset. But his focus is on something closer than yours. He sees a cow in the field between you and the sunset. The meaning you intended for that sign—sunset—is different from the meaning Joey gave it—cow. (Just think, Joey might go through life thinking that a cow is a sunset, and chances are he won't make it through veterinary school.)

LEARNING BY ASSOCIATION

Any person, infant or adult, learns through association. We learn something new by associating it with something familiar to us. However, in their world of basic survival, infants find far fewer important things than we do, and therefore need a smaller array of words or gestures. Their lives are not cluttered with the concerns that, unfortunately, fill most adults' lives. So, just what is important to infants?

During the first months of life, the important things will be limited to the essentials: the caregivers' love and touch, food, and the feelings of comfort (such as being warm and being changed). That is why, in most cases, "ma-ma" or "da-da" is the first word to come out of their mouths. You, the caregivers, are the ones who provide them with the essentials and are your infants' most important "associates" in early life.

If you start making the sound "daddy" enough times when dad walks into the room, before long your little baby Emma will associate that new sound with the big guy with a low voice who gives her love, and a bottle, and occasionally (if she's lucky) a clean diaper. Emma will learn signing exactly the same way she learns words. For example, when you make the sign **EAT** as she starts to eat, that visual symbol will soon be associated in her mind with the mushy stuff that tastes good and is fun to throw.

WILL SIGNING INTERFERE WITH MY CHILD'S SPEECH DEVELOPMENT?

Some parents have wondered whether signing would interfere with normal speech development. This is a natural concern, but you need not worry.

A considerable amount of research supports the fact that children exposed to several languages early in life achieve higher levels of language competency later on. Studies conducted at the University of California at Davis by Drs. Linda Acredolo and Susan Goodwyn determined that babies who used symbolic gestures early learned to speak more readily than those babies who did not. Their research also indicated that the signing babies scored higher in intelligence tests, understood more words, had larger vocabularies, and engaged in more sophisticated play. In their book *Baby Signs,* Acredolo and Goodwyn present their research findings and offer their approach to communicating with babies. It is an excellent resource for any parent.

In my observations, the children who used signs in their early language showed above-average understanding of English syntax earlier than those who did not use signs. Children who had not learned signing were just starting to identify objects with words, while the children in our study were already talking about those objects. The signing children had the advantage of previously learning how to identify objects, feelings, and needs through signs. The important thing is that using signs to communicate before speech develops can enhance the overall communication process.

TO CONTRIBUTE OR TO COMMIT?

A pig and a hen were walking together in the barnyard. The hen said, "Our farmer has been so good to us. We should somehow repay him for his kindness." "What do you have in mind?" asked the pig. "Well," suggested the hen, "how about serving him a fine ham and egg breakfast?" The pig thought for a moment then replied, "For you that's a contribution—for me it's a commitment!"

Learning to sign requires only that you make the hen's contribution rather than the pig's commitment. Reactions to things you and your children see, things you do, and things your children do, will now be expressed through your hands, face, and body, as well as through your voice. You will be contributing to the communication process by adding the dozen or so signs that reflect your infant's daily activities and interests. The only commitment involved is to have fun.

HOW TO SIGN WITH YOUR BABY

LET YOUR FINGERS DO THE TALKING

On page 32, I explain the first signs infants respond to quickly. Start getting familiar with those signs you will be introducing first. Try using them with other family members or friends during every-day activities. Let learning the signs be enjoyable. The last thing you want is for signing to be a burden or a chore.

With a little practice you can become spontaneous and natural with your signs. Some focused time with your infants will help you identify the various signals they send that let you know they are ready to start. By the time your children's gazes start connecting with yours, you will be ready to introduce signs.

GAZES: OPPORTUNE MOMENTS TO INTRODUCE SIGNS

As you focus on your infant's behavior and habits, you will recognize different kinds of gazes happening between you. These gazes are instances of mutual perception and are the moments to introduce signs. Try to anticipate when these gazes are about to occur, and be ready to respond with a sign. Three kinds of gazes provide good opportunities to introduce signs.

Expressive gazes happen when your infant has a need, or wants to express a feeling or ask a question.

Suppose your infant Danielle is eating some applesauce and finishes it before she has had enough. She looks to you for more. In the instant the two of you make eye contact, her expression is saying "more." This is what I call an expressive gaze. This would be a perfect time to introduce the sign **MORE?**

MORE

Chance mutual gazes happen when you and your infant look at each other at the same time by chance, or for no particular reason.

Imagine you are sitting across from your infant son, Raymond. His eyes scan the room until they meets yours. For a moment, you are connected by your gaze. Your child's attention is completely on you in that instant. This is a chance mutual gaze. At this moment, your son is receptive to whatever you communicate to him. This is a good time to introduce a sign for something in the room, like a book that you are about to read to him.

Pointed gazes happen when you and your child look at the same thing at the same time and then look at each other.

CAT

A cat walks in the room and meows. You and your daughter Nicole both look at the cat and then at each other. The instant Nicole returns her gaze to you, you make the **CAT** sign and point to the cat. *Pointed gaze* episodes will happen more frequently as you show your children additional signs for the things they see and experience.

LET'S FACE IT

During infancy, your child takes in an incredible amount of information from your facial expressions. Vivid expressions will help give your signs and words more meaning.

Adding the appropriate expression will also enhance your child's understanding of whatever you are communicating. In some cases, the face carries as much meaning as the sign or word itself. Use your face generously.

Notice in the pictures below, the sign for **LITTLE** shows the shoulders hunched and the eyes squinting. Also notice the expressions when signing **COLD** and **PAIN**. Every utterance has the potential to carry an expression.

LITTLE   **COLD**   **PAIN**

THE FIRST SIGN OF INTELLIGENT LIFE

My son Stratton was eight months old when he made his first sign. I had been showing him the sign **MORE** for a month whenever I suspected he might have been wanting more of something. On this particular evening, he was in his high chair eating dinner. He ate a few peas and then accidentally knocked the rest on the floor. He looked up at me and signed **MORE**. He made the sign as if he had been using it for a long time. He seemed to know I would understand and respond to his request.

I tried to be cool and calm, but inside I was jumping up and down. I wanted to find a balance between teaching him to be careful with his food and showing my joy that he signed his first word. Anyway, I quickly brought him some more peas. After that, he used the **MORE** sign in many appropriate situations. The smile that appeared on my face then returns each time I recall that first sign.

By the way, I occasionally voiced the word "more" at the same time I signed **MORE**. I noticed that Stratton would sometimes vocalize a sound while he made the sign. The sound evolved from a grunt to a "ma" sound over several months. Other parents experienced similar responses from their infants.

HOW TO SHOW YOUR INFANT A SIGN

The best time to introduce a sign varies according to the situation. Sometimes just *before* you do something is best. Other times showing a sign *during* an experience works well, and occasionally, showing a sign immediately *after* an occurrence will help make the association clearer. The best times to show some of the first few basic signs are explained in the sections that follow.

When you introduce signs that are not explained in the next few sections, try to get a feel for the best approach to use by interacting with your infants. Your children will eventually connect the experience to the sign. Shared meaning will be established between you and your children following several repeated episodes. After your infants' first attempts to make the sign are rewarded with the response they wanted, they will be motivated to learn more signs. Your children will hunger for signs to satisfy their ever-increasing needs, desires, and curiosities.

I recommend you sign close to your eyes the instant your child looks at you. It's important to make the sign close to your face, directly in the sight-line between you and your child.

After showing a sign for several weeks, I found it helpful to shape and move my infant's hands immediately after I made the sign. Eventually, my son would offer me his hands, wanting me to move them for him. I always made this process into a game and didn't *expect* any solo signing by him. After all, this isn't a drill, just loving play that helps him link the movements with communication. One parent remarked that it was too bad we couldn't reach into our babies' mouths and shape their tongues and teeth to help them learn to speak. However, we *can* occasionally manipulate their hands to help them form their signs.

Repeat the sign every time you show it. Reward your children's attempts to make a sign. Show your enthusiasm and repeat the sign again. I usually throw in a hug. I like hugs.

WHICH SIGNS TO START WITH AND WHEN TO START

Child psychologists have learned that toddlers typically understand the following six basic concepts and can use them early in their communication. The following list will help you identify the concepts your children will understand and the types of things for which your infants may want to learn signs.

1. naming something (milk, a dog, a book)

2. addressing someone (papa, mama, grandma)

3. finding something (where shoe?, where cat?)

4. something gone (no toy, food all gone)

5. asking for more (more milk, hide again)

6. possessing something (my bear, your sock)

Initially, everyday simple activities and needs such as eating, drinking, changing diapers, or wanting more of something are perfect opportunities to introduce signs. I suggest you start with the signs **MILK**, **MORE**, and **EAT**, which are among the simplest to make. Keep making these signs for at least a month before adding other signs. Don't overload your infant at the beginning. Stick to these basic signs until your infant starts making them. Then continue using the first few and gradually add more signs. For children older than a year, more signs may be introduced right away.

Most families participating in *Sign with your Baby* research started showing their infants signs around their children's sixth or seventh month. We also had families start with older toddlers, around eight to eleven months. You can start showing your infants signs as early or as late as you wish, but generally by their sixth or seventh month they have enough developed memory to retain a sign's image for future reference.

EAT

As you are about to feed your babies, you sign **EAT**. Show your infants the sign before each feeding time and while you are feeding them or while they are attempting to feed themselves. Eventually, as your infants learn what the sign means, they will use it when

EAT

they want to eat. Several parents mentioned that they were able to tell if their infants were hungry or not, simply by making the sign with an inquisitive expression and watching their infants' reactions.

One family was using signs with their nine-month-old daughter. The parents had been showing her signs for three months, but she hadn't signed anything yet. One day the mother said to her child, without using any signs, "Go tell daddy it's time to eat." The little nine-month-old rolled her walker over to her father, looked at him and made the **EAT** sign. This was her first sign. It's interesting how sometimes a child will suddenly start signing or talking.

MORE?

If the bottle or breast empties, or your infants run out of food, or simply stop eating, sign **MORE?** (with an inquisitive facial expression). Then allow a very slight pause before giving them more. Children sometimes associate this sign with hunger and are

MORE

likely to make the **MORE** sign when they are hungry. As their understanding becomes more sophisticated, they will differentiate between **MORE?** and **EAT**. In many families, **MORE** was the first sign their infants produced.

Shortly after my first son (at eight months) learned the sign MORE, he used it frequently. Often, when we were playing a tickle or a make-a-funny-face game and I would stop playing, he would sign MORE, MORE.

MILK

Every time your infants drink milk (whether from the breast or bottle) you show the MILK sign immediately before and after they drink.

MILK

Once your infants request milk (by making the MILK sign) and are rewarded, they will understand that their motion brings results (milk). Sometimes infants use this sign to mean anything to drink. Be aware of this and eventually offer other signs for other liquids.

Many infants make the MILK and MORE signs during their eighth or ninth month if these signs are introduced by their seventh month and repeated often during appropriate situations.

TOILET

Another sign to introduce early is **TOILET**. Show this sign when you know your infants are urinating or defecating. After some time, your children are likely to make this sign when they are wetting their diaper or moving their bowels. Eventually, they will learn to sign **TOILET** just before or while they relieve themselves.

TOILET

We found that parents used this sign more than infants did. While the infants understood the sign, they didn't initiate it very often. I believe the reason may have something to do with the newer diapers that draw the wetness away from babies' skin. These diapers are more tolerable when wet than cloth diapers. So, babies who wear new fiber diapers may find the changing experience less desirable than wearing wet diapers that don't feel wet. Those parents using cloth diapers may see their children make this sign more often, as they want the comfort of a nice dry diaper. (By the way, this is not a plug for disposable diapers.)

Showing the **TOILET** sign early can be useful in later toilet training. Your children will have a quick and easy way to tell you they have to go. This sign can also eliminate unnecessary embarrassment for an older child who has to go or who has already had an accident, but doesn't want anyone but a parent to know about it. I used this sign with my sons when they were as old as six and eight. At times, the boys would get so involved in their activities that they would ignore nature's call. I would notice their little dance and subtly motion **TOILET** to them. That would bring them back to reality—they are not Super Heroes and need a few moments to take care of business.

TOUCH-NO

Suppose you and your child Aaron are visiting a friend whose house is filled with plants. Aaron toddles about, exploring the greenery. While you are talking with your friend, Aaron discovers a plant that looks different from the others. He is extra curious

TOUCH   **NO**

about this unusual green thing, and so he touches it. As it turns out, this strange green thing is a cactus. You sign **TOUCH-NO** as you comfort Aaron and remove the cactus needles from his fingers.

It may not be a cactus, but at some time your infants will reach for something that could hurt them. The important thing is that the moment when your infants touch or are about to touch something that will cause them discomfort is the time to introduce the **TOUCH-NO** sign. However, the experience need not involve pain or discomfort. Use an object that has a rough surface (such as burlap, scratchy wool, or a sanding block); anything that is unpleasant to the tender skin of an infant will work. Touch the object and then show an expression of pain on your face and sign **TOUCH-NO**. Your curious infant will very likely try to touch, or actually touch the object, at which time you can repeat the **TOUCH-NO** sign. Your infant will eventually connect the sign **TOUCH-NO** with whatever discomfort they experience from their environment. Learning **TOUCH-NO** and using it as a warning can prevent other discomfort or even injuries.

Here is an imaginary situation that demonstrates another advantage to using **TOUCH-NO**. Let's say you and your toddler Amber, who is fourteen months old, are visiting a friend who has a dog.

Like many children, Amber is especially fond of trying to pull out the hair on every furry little animal she sees. You say to her in words, "Don't bother the dog over there." Amber sees you pointing at the dog. The only word in your sentence she understands may be "dog." In her excitement of recognizing the word "dog," she may very well run up to the dog and point at its face (or try to pluck the little fella hairless) to show you she understands "dog"—which, of course, is exactly what you were trying to avoid.

This kind of miscommunication can be prevented by understanding how your children learn language. Then you can adjust your communication to fit their way of perceiving the world. It is better to simply identify the object and give a command than it is to supply them with a complex sentence containing only one or two words they can understand. If the sign **TOUCH-NO** were already understood, it would have been more effective to sign **DOG**, **TOUCH-NO** as you say to her, "Don't touch the dog."

Those parents who introduced the **TOUCH-NO** sign early in their children's lives are glad they did; their toddlers understood and usually followed this warning.

In most cases, children don't produce **TOUCH-NO**—it's a caregiver's command. Some children did produce the **TOUCH** sign and then look to their parents for approval. Several parents told me they saw their toddlers sign **TOUCH-NO** to other children, warning them of danger.

HOT, WARM, AND COLD

HOT and **COLD** are useful signs and can be introduced during feeding time. For example, you have a dish of food that is too hot to eat. The steam is still rising as you set it on the table out of reach of your toddler. You point to the food and sign **HOT**. The steam rising from food gives your child something visual to associate with hot.

HOT

WARM

A warm bowl of water next to a cool bowl of water is a good way to introduce **WARM** and **COLD**. Experiment with each bowl, allowing your children to feel the water, then show them the appropriate sign.

COLD

"CAN YOU TELL ME WHERE IT HURTS?"

Signing offers this unique benefit: it provides a way for your children to tell you where they are hurt. When they come to you crying, show them the **PAIN** sign as you console them. Make the sign at the injured area. After a short time, your infants will associate pain with this sign. Once they learn the relationship between an injury and the **PAIN** sign, the stage is set for locating their pain.

PAIN/HURT   **WHERE**

It's interesting that when asked **WHERE PAIN?**, some children point to the object that hurt them rather than showing where they are hurt on their bodies.

When your children are hurt and you have no idea what happened or where they are hurt, you can use the **PAIN-WHERE?-SEARCH** sequence. You sign **PAIN**, and then **WHERE?** Then sign **SEARCH** as you move the **SEARCH** sign around their bodies. I found it helpful to sign **PAIN-WHERE?** then touch my son's head, and sign **PAIN** there? (pointing to a spot). I would go over his whole body in this way until he nodded his head, yes. This process was successful in locating the injury with many children.

SEARCH

After a few episodes of searching for the pain, your child will get the message and direct you to the injured area without going through the entire search process. The search-for-a-shoe game discussed later is a good way to introduce the **WHERE** and **SEARCH** signs.

Kim was 14 months, and playing in the park, when she stumbled and fell. Her mother jumped up from her bench, looked at Kim and signed **HURT?** Kim shook her head "no" and went on playing. Later, when they had returned home, Kim was playing with her rag doll. She fell again, this time landing on her doll. She picked up the doll and went over to her mother. Kim looked sad, so her mother asked if she was hurt, by signing **HURT?** Kim set her doll down and signed **HURT** over the doll. Her mother got a bandage and put it on the doll. Kim picked up her doll and walked away happy.

SOME HANDY GAMES

Be creative and spontaneous with signing. Many signs can be used while playing games. **HIDE**, **SEARCH**, **CATCH**, and **TICKLE** are some obvious ones. With three or more people, play hide and seek using the signs **HIDE**, **SEARCH**, **WHERE**, and **TICKLE**. One person hides and the other person goes with the toddler and signs **WHERE** and **SEARCH** while looking for the hidden person. When you find the hidden person, you tickle them. This may also be a good time to show the **CATCH** sign.

HIDE   **SEARCH**   **WHERE**

CATCH   **TICKLE**

Older toddlers, about 14 to 18 months, will love this next game. While they are looking at you, put a toy or something special to them out of sight, but within a few crawls or steps. Sign **WHERE?** with an inquisitive look on your face. Your toddlers look for the object and when they find it, you give them a hug. Repeat the game, finding a different hiding place each time. You may try signing **SEARCH** during the search process, moving the sign in the direction you are searching.

One family invented a game they called "catch the worm." The mother cut off the index finger of an old glove and attached little eyes and a fuzzy pipe cleaner to make it look like a worm or caterpillar. Wearing the worm on her index finger, she would sign **WORM** to her daughter.

WORM

As her finger moved across the front of her hand, her infant would try to catch the worm. Each time the child caught the worm, the worm would interact with her and she would get a hug. This is one example of the limitless games you can create with signs and your imagination.

I read lots of animal books with pictures to my sons and would make the signs for the animals as we came to them. Eventually this evolved into a game. As we saw the picture, I would say the name, make the animal's sound, and then sign its name. This became very useful when we went to the zoo. I would sign the individual animals as we watched them. My sons would also make the sign for the animals and imitate the sounds I made.

The vocabulary section includes the signs for alligator, bear, bee, bird, bull, butterfly, cat, cow, dog, elephant, fish, fly, frog, horse, insect, lion, monkey, mosquito, mouse, rabbit, snake, spider, squirrel, turtle, and worm. (Let me know what sound you come up with for a worm.)

RECOGNIZING YOUR CHILDREN'S SIGNS

Children may not always make a sign exactly as you make it. Motor skills develop at different rates. Therefore, dexterity levels will vary among children of the same age.

WHERE
(YOUNGER CHILD)

WHERE
(OLDER CHILD)

Notice the difference between the way these children make the **WHERE** sign. The first child points both index fingers and makes the motion with one hand, using the other as a support. The older child signs **WHERE** the correct way except his motion is wider.

Remember, although your children will try their best to imitate your movements, their hand shapes will be crude at first. Keep making the signs correctly, despite your children's variations. They need to see the signs repeated the right way, just as they need to hear words pronounced correctly to perfect their speech.

When my sons were first learning signs, they would offer me their hands so I could help them make the sign *movements*. As they grew older, I helped them form the specific *finger shapes*.

Here is another example of variations in the way children may form a sign. The first picture shows the way a child at ten months signed **WATER** by holding up only his index finger. The second picture shows the way the same child at thirteen months made the sign correctly—holding up all three fingers.

WATER
(EARLIER VERSION)

WATER
(LATER VERSION)

My sons were learning to sign in rural Alaska, where many small planes flew overhead. So **AIRPLANE** was a sign they learned early.

AIRPLANE

When an airplane passed over, I would look up and point at the plane. I would sign **AIRPLANE** and move my hand in the same direction as the plane. I also made a "rrrrmmmm" sound. Then, I would say the word "airplane." At ten and a half months, Stratton used his pointed index finger and moved it over his head making a "rrrrmmmm" sound. Damian, at eleven months, used his fist with the same movement and said "appp."

I remember the first time I introduced the airplane sign to Damian. Later the same day he made the sign and sound several times. He was reaffirming his understanding that the sign represented the airplane. This also indicated that he was thinking about the plane and wanted to talk about it. I realized that he wanted to initiate conversation. Learning the sign **AIRPLANE** gave him an opportunity to do this. It was the first time he was able to start a conversation based on an experience we had shared. I reinforced his attempt to discuss the airplane by making the sign. Then I acted out an animated version of the event— it was loud, it flew high over the trees, and then it disappeared in the distance. I had the same experience with both boys, in which signs enabled them to initiate conversation.

A mother who started signing by using the **MORE** sign told me that her six month infant clapped her hands when she wanted something.   This child's clapping—which can be seen as babbling in signs—eventually became **MORE** as her fingers were able to form the exact shape.

Your child's signs will go through a metamorphosis, sometimes changing over days or weeks. The vocabulary section has space where you can identify your baby's unique sign variations.

REPEATING AND REINFORCING YOUR SIGNS

Have fun with your whole family using your signs at every possible opportunity. It's advantageous to use signs among all family members so your babies see consistent manual communication in their surroundings. Your children are making a connection between the sign and what it represents. This connection is reinforced every time they see or make the sign. Show caregivers, such as babysitters, the signs your infants use. It may be frustrating for your children if the people who care for them don't understand the signs your children make.

My research showed that some children respond quickly to some signs and more slowly to others. The age at which each child produces a sign is completely individual. Be patient and consistent. Never stop providing a sign just because you think they know it (you've seen them sign it a few times) or because they don't sign it at all. Keep using the signs. Whatever happens, don't show frustration. This is supposed to be fun for you and your babies. If you let them feel that you are disappointed or impatient, they will lose interest and the fun could end.

Set up situations that offer the opportunity to use a sign. During meal times, give your children half as much food as usual and then sign **MORE?** when they finish the first portion.

ALL-GONE

Also, when your infants finish something on their plates, you can sign **ALL-GONE**. By the way, this sign will soon become handy when you don't want them to have more of something. Infants also use this sign to tell you they are finished with something.

Always be prepared to acknowledge your child's attempts to produce signs. Don't wait until your child produces one sign before you introduce another. Use your daily experiences to direct you in the vocabulary you generate.

One thing that really surprised me was that my children would remember and produce signs after not seeing or using them for weeks. My son Stratton was fifteen months old and for several days we kept meeting people with infants.

I showed Stratton the sign for **BABY** each time. He never made the sign himself until three weeks later when we saw another baby. He looked at the baby, then made the **BABY** sign to me.

BABY

Other parents were also amazed at their children's capability for retention. However, do not make the mistake of relying entirely on your child's memory, phenomenal as it may be. You should repeat your signs at every opportunity.

Anticipate your child's needs and use signs throughout your day. Make it a pleasant experience for both of you. Add new signs when the appropriate situation arises.

COMBINING SIGNS

After your children have made a sign several times, you can begin combining it with a new sign or one they already know: **MORE-MILK**, **FOOD-ALL GONE**, **PAPA-DANCE**, **COLD-WATER**, **WHERE-SHOES**, etc.

TOUCH-NO and **HURT** go well together. Many children respond quickly to this combination.

Children will sometimes sign **WHERE-MOTHER** or **WHERE-FATHER** if either parent is not in sight. **WHERE** can be used before many objects or people.

HOW TO CREATE A NEW SIGN

Occasionally, something will make an impression on your child and you will want a sign for it but will not find it in the vocabulary section of this book. When this happens you can invent a sign. Make your sign so it mimics an action or shows an object's shape. Be spontaneous when inventing a sign. Create a sign that visually represents the object or situation. Try to recreate the most dramatic characteristic with your hands.

For example, playing an instrument can be imitated once your child sees it being played. Keep the movement simple. Add a facial expression to your sign when it's appropriate.

I suggest you create a sign for each person (or pet) who has regular contact with your child, or for a person whose photograph your child sees regularly. I try to come up with a motion that shows an obvious characteristic of the person (or animal).

Record the new signs you invent and describe their origins. We left space for notes under each term in the vocabulary section. Enter your own signs alphabetically. This will help you and others locate them later. Remember, your child will get confused if you change the way you make a sign from day to day.

The *Sign with your Baby Quick Reference Guide,* included in the Complete Learning Kit (ref. page 109), is also a valuable resource to help you document when you have shown and when your child has produced many of the most useful signs. It's a great tool to help you quickly learn the signs and to teach other caregivers the signs your baby knows.

The signs in this book are American Sign Language (ASL) signs. I also demonstrate each of these signs in the last segment of the *Sign with your Baby Training Video.* During the demonstration segment, the video displays a digital counter on-screen to help you locate specific hand shapes and signs. An index of hand shapes and an index of signs and their corresponding video counter numbers appear on pages 55 and 57 of this book. If you would like to use ASL signs for words not included in this book and video, you may wish to locate an ASL dictionary.

THE POWER OF SILENCE

It's natural to want to say the corresponding words with your signs. Vocalizing is almost automatic and you may be tempted to do it all the time. However, you can help develop your child's visual and analytic senses by maintaining a balance between verbal communication and silent eye-to-eye communication. I suggest you maintain some silent interaction. Senses are stimulated in different ways during silent communication. Children draw on other resources and develop different skills when their oral/aural channels take a rest.

THINGS TO REMEMBER

- It's never too late to begin signing. You can even use signs after your toddler begins speaking. Signing will enhance your communication and add an element of fun to your lives.

- Parents can start using signs as early as the seventh month. However, understand that a child may not produce a sign until their eighth or ninth month or beyond.

- Get familiar with the first few signs you will use. Many parents have had great success with the signs **MORE**, **MILK**, and **EAT** as their first signs.

- Show your infant signs at every opportunity and be consistent in the way you make your signs.

- After you use the first few signs for a couple of months, introduce more signs, such as the signs for things that interest your infant (a pet, a person) or an object your infant sees often (shoes, a teddy bear, or a book).

- Make your signs in the sight-line, and be ready to use a sign during *chance mutual gazes*, *expressive gazes*, and *pointed gazes*.

- Begin playing signing games such as "hide and seek" and "catch the worm" with your infants.

- When your infants attempt their first signs, encourage them and help them shape their hands.

- Learn more signs and be ready to introduce them at any opportunity or create opportunities to show new signs.

- Always repeat each sign you show. In general, the more your infants see a sign, the faster they will learn it and use it.

- Be patient. Never show disappointment or frustration if your child does not produce a sign. All children are different and need to be treated according to their own timetables and behaviors.

- Have fun!

THE TERRIBLE TWOS AND THREES: TALK YOUR CHILD OUT OF THEM

Where do the "terrible twos and threes" come from, anyway? How could those little angels turn into such testing bundles of mischief? What is the easiest way to navigate through these years?

Maybe two- or three-year-olds are feeling frustrated because they have just spent their entire lives unable to communicate what they understood or needed. They may have been thinking, "I know what's going on, but why don't you know that I know?" So, when toddlers do gain some verbal power, maybe they need to release—it's pay-back time. I suspect the "terrible twos and threes" are due not only to the child testing limits, but also to the absence of or the breakdown in clear communication.

Remember the imaginary scenario of your toddler Juliet and her hurt nose? Without signs, you both would have felt frustrated. It could have been a terrible experience for you because you wanted so much to understand and help her. It would have been equally frustrating for Juliet because she had something to express and no way to express it.

FINAL THOUGHTS

Young children have little or no control over their lives. Communication is one thing that begins to empower them. You the caregivers are the most important influences in your toddlers' worlds. Communication with you at an early age will feed them emotionally and intellectually. More and more research confirms what wise parents have always known— you will establish the lasting foundation of your child's physical, mental, and spiritual health by meeting all these needs during those first few years. And naturally, the time you share with your child will be of higher quality when you are more interactive.

My own children are in school now and signing continues to enrich our interaction (from time to time). With non-verbal communication, our eyes tend to look a little deeper to understand each other. This process leads to a closer sense of connection. I feel that by experiencing communication in this way, you tap a little deeper into the roots of parent/child bonding—the more dynamic your communication, the stronger your bond.

As a parent, signing gives me an incredible satisfaction. I hope you enjoy signing with your baby and benefit from it as I and others have. Many who have used this system have expressed the delight they experienced communicating with their children so early in their children's lives. Many parenting rewards are built on a foundation of good communication.

As my sons and other young signers grew older, we discovered that using the hands to talk actually helped our children develop a strong foundation for spoken language. We found that our children expressed themselves clearly when speech began. By clearly, I mean they were able to choose or search for the precise words to express their thoughts. They followed a logical and systematic pattern in expressing themselves. I also noticed that my sons would often rely on me to provide them with the right word for whatever they were trying to say.

This process would follow the same pattern as the way in which I had introduced a sign for an object or situation. Many children continue to use signs after they begin speaking because it's so much fun.

While I still have your attention, I'd like to offer a couple of suggestions. When your children begin to speak, they will learn and use whatever words you give them. Don't underestimate their intelligence and memory. Use correct and accurate words. Even if they cannot pronounce a word perfectly, they have heard it and will eventually use it in the correct context.

I taught my sons the specific words for injuries (bruise, cut, scrape, etc.). They learned to distinguish the different types of injuries, while I noticed other children their ages still said "ouch" or "owie" for all injuries. This is just an example; you can carry this idea through all vocabulary development. Teaching your children a "baby" word for something, only to replace it later with a more sophisticated word, may be doing them a disservice.

One last bit of advice: I know some parents who, with all good intentions, want to be such good parents that they over anticipate and meet their children's every need too readily. The drawback here is that these children rarely have an opportunity to express their needs. Sometime between the first indication of need and the screaming stage is the opportunity to introduce signs. This way, you can be most effective in helping your infants develop their ability to tell you exactly what they want.

Also, don't ask your children to sign out of context, perform for others, or compare your children to other children. Be careful not to show disappointment if your child chooses not to sign in a particular situation even if your child has signed in a similar situation before. Remember, don't make signing with your baby a lesson, but use signs in your daily life as an augmentation to your speech. Don't teach the signs, just sign. Let your baby discover.

HAND   SHAPES

These numbers will help you quickly locate a hand shape in the training video by finding the corresponding number displayed on-screen in the video's demonstration segment.

1 Hand 0:01	Bent 5 Hand 0:19	C Hand 0:40	X Hand 1:00
2 Hand 0:04	6 Hand 0:22	O Hand 0:44	Modified X Hand . 1:04
Inverted 2 Hand ... 0:07	Modified 8 Hand . 0:26	S Hand 0:48	Y Hand 1:08
Bent 2 Hand 0:11	9 Hand 0:30	T Hand 0:52	Cupped Hand 1:12
5 Hand 0:15	A Hand 0:36	Flat O Hand 0:56	Claw Hand 1:16

These hand shapes, borrowed from American Sign Language, are used to form the signs in the vocabulary section.

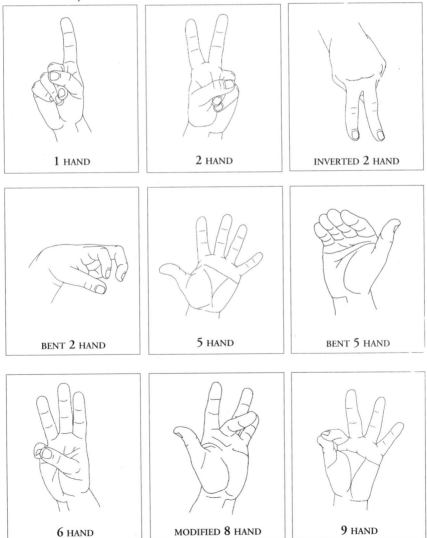

1 HAND	2 HAND	INVERTED 2 HAND
BENT 2 HAND	5 HAND	BENT 5 HAND
6 HAND	MODIFIED 8 HAND	9 HAND

A HAND

C HAND

O HAND

S HAND

T HAND

FLAT O HAND

X HAND

MODIFIED X HAND

Y HAND

CUPPED HAND

CLAW HAND

VOCABULARY

These numbers will help you quickly locate a sign in the training video by finding the corresponding number displayed on-screen in the video's demonstration segment.

Again 1:26	Delicious 4:26	Hurt 7:15	Sick 10:22
Airplane 1:29	Dirty 4:31	I Love You (1) 7:20	Sister 10:28
All Gone 1:35	Dog 4:35	I Love You (2) 7:23	Sit 10:32
Alligator 1:40	Down 4:40	Ice Cream 7:27	Sleep 10:37
Apple 1:46	Dream 4:44	In 7:33	Snake 10:42
Baby 1:51	Drink 4:48	Insect 7:37	Snow 10:47
Banana 1:57	Earache 4:52	Jump 7:42	Socks 10:52
Bath 2:02	Eat 4:58	Ketchup 7:48	Sore Throat 10:56
Bear 2:07	Elephant 5:03	Lion 7:53	Sorry 11:02
Beautiful 2:11	Fall Down 5:07	Little 7:58	Spider 11:07
Bed 2:16	Father 5:11	Meat 8:03	Spoon 11:12
Bee 2:22	Finished 5:16	Milk 8:08	Squirrel 11:17
Big 2:26	Fire 5:19	Mine 8:14	Stomachache 11:22
Bird 2:31	Fish 5:23	Monkey 8:19	Stop 11:28
Book 2:36	Flower 5:28	Moon 8:25	Sun 11:32
Bottle 2:40	Fly 5:33	More 8:30	Telephone 11:37
Boy 2:46	Friend 5:38	Mosquito 8:36	Tell 11:41
Bread 2:51	Frog 5:43	Mother 8:41	Thank You 11:46
Brother 2:56	Get 5:48	Mouse 8:45	Throw 11:50
Bull 3:00	Girl 5:52	No 8:49	Thunder 11:54
Burn 3:05	Go 5:58	Orange 8:55	Tickle 11:59
Butter 3:09	Good 6:02	Out 9:00	Tired 12:04
Butterfly 3:14	Grandfather 6:07	Over 9:05	Toilet 12:09
Cake 3:19	Grandmother 6:12	Pain 9:10	Touch 12:14
Car 3:24	Happy 6:17	Pie 9:15	Turtle 12:18
Cat 3:29	Head 6:22	Play 9:20	Under 12:24
Catch 3:34	Headache 6:27	Please 9:25	Up 12:28
Change 3:39	Hear 6:32	Popcorn 9:30	Wait 12:33
Clean 3:44	Hello 6:37	Potato 9:35	Want 12:38
Clouds 3:49	Help (1) 6:40	Rabbit 9:40	Warm 12:42
Coat 3:54	Help (2) 6:43	Rain 9:46	Water 12:46
Cold 3:58	Hide 6:46	Run 9:51	Where 12:52
Cookie 4:02	Home 6:50	Saxophone 9:55	Work 12:58
Corn-on-the-cob .. 4:07	Horse 6:55	Scared 10:02	Worm 13:02
Cow 4:13	Hot 7:01	Search 10:06	Yes 13:09
Cry 4:16	House 7:05	Share 10:12	You're Welcome 13:14
Dance 4:22	Hug 7:10	Shoes 10:17	

MOVEMENT   INDICATORS

SINGLE MOVEMENT	DOUBLE MOVEMENT	MULTIPLE MOVEMENT

AGAIN

The cupped action hand arcs down and the fingertips touch the palm of the flat base hand.

AIRPLANE

The "Y" hand, with the index finger extended and palm down, moves through space to show the flight of an airplane.

ALL GONE

The flat base hand is held face down. The "5" hand rests on top then slides down the fingers of the base hand and closes into an "S" hand.

ALLIGATOR

Top and bottom claw hands touch at the wrists. Then the palms touch and the fingers interlace. This motion is repeated, like an alligator's jaws opening and closing.

APPLE

The index finger of the "X" hand touches the cheek while the hand twists.

BABY

One arm cradles the other and both move from side to side, as if rocking a baby.

BANANA

The base hand is in the "1" position. The modified "X" hand slides down the side of the "1" index finger several times, as if peeling a banana.

BATH

Both "A" hands rub against the body in circular motions, as though washing the body.

BEAR

Two claw hands are crossed facing inward in front of the chest, making a clawing movement.

BEAUTIFUL

A "5" hand begins on one side of the face, and circles around the face, closing to a flat "O" hand at the chin.

BED

The tilted head is placed on two flat palms held together at the cheek, as if the head were lying on a pillow.

BEE

The "9" action hand touches the corner of the upper lip. Then the same hand takes a "B" position and brushes across the mouth, as if brushing away a bee.

BIG

Both hands, in a bent "L" shape, start in front of the chest and move out to the sides.

BIRD

The index finger and thumb are held together at the lips. They snap open and closed, like a bird's beak.

BOOK

Two flat hands are held together, and then open.

BOTTLE

The flat base hand is held palm up. The "C" action hand taps the base hand several times.

BOY

The hand closes to a flat "O" at forehead, as if grabbing a baseball cap.

BREAD

The base hand is held palm facing body and the open cupped action hand brushes up and down on the back of the base hand several times.

BROTHER

The "L" action hand is held to the forehead, then brought down to the "L" base hand.

BULL

The index fingers of the "S" hands extend forward at the temples, representing a bull's horns.

BURN

The base hand is held palm down at chest level. The "5" action hand is held beneath the base hand, with the fingers wiggling to represent flames.

BUTTER

The base hand is held palm up and the first two fingers brush the palm, as if spreading butter.

BUTTERFLY

With the palms facing down, the thumbs lock together and the hands flap up and down, like butterfly wings.

CAKE

The "5" base hand is palm up. The claw action hand touches the base palm and moves up slowly several inches, like a cake rising.

CAR

Both "S" hands are
held out at chest level,
moving in opposite
arc motions, as if
steering a car.

CAT

The "9" hand touches
the corner of the upper
lip, brushing out and
away from the face
several times,
representing a cat's
whiskers.

CATCH

The open "5" action
hand swoops down
and catches the "1"
base hand index
finger.

CHANGE

Two "A" hands are held at chest level with the knuckles of one hand resting on the knuckles of the other hand. Both hands pivot in opposite directions to switch places.

CLEAN

The base hand is held flat with palm facing up. The "A" action hand rubs against the base palm in a circular motion, as if scrubbing or cleaning.

CLOUDS

Both "5" hands are held at eye level, with the palms facing out. The palms turn inward together with small circular motions, as if the hands were outlining clouds.

COAT

Both "A" hands are held at shoulder level then come together in front of the chest, as if closing a coat.

COLD

Both "S" hands are held close to the body at shoulder level with the shoulders hunched and the arms shaking.

COOKIE

The base "5" hand is held palm facing the side. The claw action hand twists around and back again against the palm, making the shape of a cookie.

CORN-ON-THE-COB

Both claw hands are held in front of the mouth, palms facing each other. The hands pivot back and forth, as if turning a cob of corn.

COW

The thumb of the "Y" hand taps the temple several times.

CRY

The index fingers of both "1" hands slide down the cheeks, showing the paths of tears.

DANCE

The "5" base hand is held with the palm facing up. The inverted "2" hand swings back and forth over the base hand, as if dancing.

DELICIOUS

The "8" hand is held with the middle finger touching the lips, and the hand pivots out and from face.

DIRTY

The back of the "5" hand is held under the chin with the fingers wiggling.

DOG

The middle finger
snaps against the
thumb, as if calling
a dog. You can also pat
your front thigh
several times.

DOWN

The index finger
points downward
several times.

DREAM

The index finger of the
"1" hand touches the
side of the head, then
bends and straightens
as it moves away from
the head.

DRINK

The "C" hand is held with the thumb at the lower lip, pivoting up.

EARACHE

Both "1" hands tap together several times in front of the ear.

EAT

The flat "O" hand taps the mouth several times.

ELEPHANT

The "C" hand starts at the nose, then slides down in front of the body, representing an elephant's trunk.

FALL DOWN

The base hand is held with palm facing up. The "inverted 2" hand moves from a "standing" position to a "lying" position, representing someone falling.

FATHER

The "5" hand is held up with the thumb tapping the forehead several times.

FINISHED

Both "5" hands are
held palms up, then
the palms flip down in
a swift motion.

FIRE

Both "5" hands are
held with the palms
facing body, and the
fingers wiggle as the
hands slowly rise.

FISH

The flat base hand is
held sideways with the
fingertips touching the
flat action hand at the
wrist. The action hand
moves forward,
wiggling slightly, like
a fish swimming.

FLOWER

The flat "O" hand touches one side of the nose and then the other.

FLY

The base arm is held with the elbow bent. The claw action hand sweeps down to touch the base arm and closes into an "S" hand, as if catching a fly.

FRIEND

The index fingers lock together. Then the hands flip over and the index fingers lock the other way.

FROG

The "2" hand is held palm down under the chin, then the fingers bend and flick off of the thumb. The final position is shown with the fingers outstretched.

GET

The "5" hands are held palms facing inward, one hand above the other. Both hands close as they move toward the body.

GIRL

The thumb draws a line from the jaw to the chin.

GO

Both "1" hands bend at the wrists and point in the direction one is going.

GOOD

The fingertips of the flat hand touch the lips, then the hand moves down and away from the body.

GRANDFATHER

The "5" hand is held with the thumb to the forehead, and then makes a double arc down and away from the forehead.

GRANDMOTHER

The "5" hand is held with the thumb to the chin, and then makes a double arc down and away from the chin.

HAPPY

The flat hand pats the chest repeatedly with an upward movement, like the heart beating.

HEAD

The flat hand taps the side of the head.

HEADACHE

Both "1" hands tap together several times in front of the forehead.

HEAR

Slightly cupped action hand is placed behind the ear as if listening.

HELLO

The "5" hand waves back and forth.

HELP (1)

The "S" hand is placed on top of the flat base hand, and both rise together in this position, as if the base hand is helping lift the fist.

HELP (2)

This sign is used with younger children and is not an ASL sign. Both flat hands pat the chest.

HIDE

With hunched shoulders, the cupped action hand is palm down over the base "A" hand to "hide" it, leaving only the thumb tip "peeking out."

HOME

The flat "O" hand touches the fingertips to the chin and moves toward the ear.

HORSE

The closed "2" hand with the thumb extended touches the side of the forehead, with the fingers waving up and down.

HOT

The claw hand is held with the palm facing the mouth, then turned and dropped downwards, while mouthing "HHHH."

HOUSE

The fingertips of both flat hands join to make a roof angle. Then the flat hands separate with the palms facing, to represent the walls.

HUG

The hands grasp the upper arms, as if hugging yourself.

HURT

The index fingers of the "1" hands tap together several times at the location of the hurt area.

I LOVE YOU (1)

The "1" hand points to yourself, indicating "I." The "A" hands cross over the chest, indicating "love." The "1" hand points, indicating "you."

I LOVE YOU (2)

The "Y" hand is held up with the index finger extended.

ICE CREAM

The "S" hand moves up and down in front of the mouth, as if licking an ice cream cone.

IN

The flat "O" action
hand is placed into the
sideways "C" hand.

INSECT

The "3" hand is held
with the thumb
touching the nose.
The two fingers wiggle
together.

JUMP

The inverted "2"
action hand rests on
the palm of the base
hand. The action
hand springs up, as
if jumping.

KETCHUP

The base "S" hand is held on its side. The "5" hand strikes the top of the base hand several times, as if striking the bottom of a ketchup bottle.

LION

The claw hand is raised to the opposite side of the head and arcs around the face, outlining a lion's mane.

LITTLE

The two flat hands face each other, moving slightly in and out, to indicate a small size.

MEAT

The index finger and thumb grip the "5" hand near the last joint of the thumb, on the "meaty" part of the hand.

MILK

The claw hand, held on its side, squeezes into the "S" hand several times, as if milking a cow.

MINE

The flat hand touches the chest.

MONKEY

The hands scratch up and down at the sides, imitating a monkey.

MOON

The hand is held up with the index finger and thumb forming a "C." The eyes look toward the hand, as if gazing up at the moon.

MORE

The two "flat O" hands tap their fingertips together several times.

MOSQUITO

The "9" action hand touches the base forearm, then takes a "5" shape and slaps the forearm, as if slapping a mosquito.

MOTHER

The thumb of the "5" hand taps the chin several times.

MOUSE

The "1" hand is held up with the index finger brushing across the nose.

NO

The first two fingers
close down to touch
the extended thumb
several times.

ORANGE

The claw hand closes
several times, as if
squeezing an orange.

OUT

The fingertips of the
"flat O" action hand
are inserted in the
sideways "C" hand.
The action hand is
pulled out.

OVER

The flat base hand is held palm down while the flat action hand, with the palm facing the body, arcs over the base hand.

PAIN

The index fingers of the "1" hand tap together several times at the location of the pain.

PIE

The flat base hand is held with the palm up. The flat action hand makes two slicing motions, as if slicing a pie.

PLAY

The "Y" hands are held at the sides and pivot back and forth at the wrists.

PLEASE

The flat hand touches the chest and moves in a circular motion.

POPCORN

The modified "X" hands alternately "pop" into the "1" hand position.

POTATO

The base "S" hand is horizontal and the bent "2" action hand taps the back of the base hand several times, like a hoe digging a potato.

RABBIT

The first two fingers are held up with palms facing behind you and the fingers quiver like rabbit ears.

RAIN

The "5" hands are held at head level with the palms down. The hands drop down at a slight angle, like rain falling in the wind.

RUN

Both "L" hands are in front of the chest with the index finger of the rear hand linking to the thumb of the forward hand. Both hands move toward the body and the forward index finger bends.

SAXOPHONE

Both hands are in the claw position, with the fingers moving, and the cheeks puffed, as if playing a saxophone. Any instrument can be mimed.

SCARED

Both "S" hands are held with the palms facing each other. Then suddenly, as they move toward each other, they open to "5" hands with the fingers shaking.

SEARCH

The "C" hand passes
in front of the face in
circular motions.

SHARE

The flat base hand is
vertical with the thumb
extended upward. The
flat action hand is also
vertical and slides back
and forth across the
index finger of the
base hand.

SHOES

The two sideways "S"
hands tap together
several times.

SICK

One "8" hand touches the forehead and the other "8" hand touches the stomach.

SISTER

The "L" hand thumb touches the chin and then moves down to meet the lower "L" hand.

SIT

The first two fingers of one hand "sit" on the first two fingers of the other hand.

SLEEP

The "5" hand is held in front of the face and the eyes shut as the fingers close into a "flat O" at the chin.

SNAKE

The bent "2" hand moves forward in small arching motions.

SNOW

The "5" hands come down slowly with the fingers wiggling.

SOCKS

Both "1" hands are pointing down, one higher than the other. The fingers move up and down, brushing each other as they pass.

SORE THROAT

The "1" hands tap fingertips together several times at the throat.

SORRY

The "S" hand moves in a circular motion on the chest.

SPIDER

With crossed wrists, both claw hands face down, with the little fingers interlocked. The hands slowly move forward with the fingers wiggling like legs.

SPOON

The first two fingers sweep down to the cupped base hand and up to the mouth, as if using a spoon.

SQUIRREL

The bent "2" hands tap together several times at the fingertips.

STOMACH ACHE

The index fingers tap together several times at the stomach.

STOP

The flat base hand is held palm up and the flat action hand comes down on its side, striking the base palm.

SUN

The "C" hand is held up, and the eyes look up at the hand.

TELEPHONE

The "Y" hand is held up to the ear and mouth as if using a phone receiver.

TELL

The "1" hand touches the lips and moves out toward the person being addressed.

THANK YOU

The fingertips of the flat hand touch the lips and the hand falls forward, toward the person being thanked.

THROW

The "flat O" hand is raised and drawn toward the body then quickly moves forward and opens into a "5" hand.

THUNDER

The index finger points to the ear, and then both "S" hands are held at chest level and move alternately in and out.

TICKLE

The "1" hand wiggles at the side, as if tickling.

TIRED

Both cupped hands are held with the palms facing the body, fingertips touching the chest. The hands pivot down.

TOILET

The "T" hand shakes slightly back and forth, pivoting at the elbow.

TOUCH

The "8" hand taps the back of the flat base hand one or two times.

TURTLE

The cupped hand is held over the top of the "A" hand, representing a turtle in its shell. The thumb of the "A" hand wiggles to show the turtle's head moving.

UNDER

The cupped base hand is held palm down. The flat action hand moves down underneath the base hand.

UP

The "1" hand points upward several times.

WAIT

Both "5" hands are
held to one side with
palms up, and the
fingers wiggle.

WANT

Both flat hands are
held with palms facing
up, then the hands
form claw shapes as
they move in slightly
toward the body.

WARM

The "A" hand is held
in front of the mouth
with the fingers falling
forward one at a time,
from the index finger
to the little finger.

WATER

The index finger of the "6" hand taps the side of the mouth twice.

WHERE

The "1" hand waves from side to side, pivoting at the wrist.

WORK

One "S" hand taps the top of the other "S" hand several times at the wrist.

WORM

The palm of the flat base hand faces to the side. The index finger of the action hand is placed in the palm. The index finger curls and straightens as it moves across the palm like a worm crawling.

YES

The "S" hand moves up and down at the wrist, like a head nodding.

YOU'RE WELCOME

The flat open hand moves gracefully from in front of the face to the waist.

REFERENCES

Acredolo, L., and S. Goodwyn. (1996). <u>Baby Signs</u>. Chicago: Contemporary Books.

Bolinger, D. (1975). <u>Aspects of Language</u>. New York: Harcourt Brace Jovanovich.

Brown, R. (1973). <u>A First Language: The Early Stages</u>. Cambridge: Harvard University Press.

Bruner, J. (1983). <u>Child's Talk: Learning to Use Language</u>. New York: W. W. Norton and Company.

Bryant, P. (1974). <u>Perception and Understanding in Young Children: An Experimental Approach</u>. New York: Basic Books.

Bullowa, M., ed. (1979). <u>Before Speech: The Beginning of Interpersonal Communication</u>. New York: Cambridge University Press.

Field, T. M. and T. A. Walden. (1982). "Production and Perception of Facial Expressions in Infancy and Early Childhood." *Advances in Child Development and Behavior.* 16 (1982): 171-211.

Lieberman, P. (1984). <u>The Biology and Evolution of Language</u>. Cambridge: Harvard University Press.

Moore, T. E., ed. (1973). <u>Cognitive Development and the Acquisition of Language</u>. New York: Academic Press.

Nelson, K. (1986). <u>Event Knowledge: Structure and Function in Development</u>. Hillsdale: Lawrence Erlbaum Associates.

Nelson, K. (1985). <u>Making Sense: The Acquisition of Shared Meaning</u>. New York: Academic Press.

Wieman, J. M. and R. P. Harrison, eds. (1983). <u>Nonverbal Interaction</u>. Beverly Hills: Sage Publications.

INDEX

Acredolo, Linda 24

American Sign Language
(ASL) 13, 49

Anecdotes
    airplane 45
    eat 32-33
    more 29
    pain/hurt 11-12, 41
    touch-no 36-37

Bonding 10, 52

Cognitive Skills 20-21

Deaf, the 13-14

Early Child Language
Acquisition 10, 13

Facial Expressions .. 9, 28, 33

Games 41-43, 51

Gazes 26-27, 50
    chance mutual 27, 50
    expressive 27, 50
    pointed 27, 50

Goodwyn, Susan 24

Intelligence............ 9, 14, 17,
.... 19, 24, 53

Johnson, Dr. Eugene ... 20-21

Motor Skills 18, 20-21

Shared Meaning 21-22, 30

Sight-Line 30, 50

Signs
    airplane...................... 45
    all-gone 47, 48
    baby 47
    cat 28
    cold 28, 38, 39, 48
    catch 41, 42
    dance 48
    dog 38

eat/food 18, 23,
.... 32, 33, 48, 50

father/papa 48

hide 41

hot............................ 38

little 28

milk 32, 34, 48, 50

more 27, 29, 32,
.... 33, 34, 46, 48, 50

mother....................... 48

pain/hurt 28, 39, 40,
.... 41, 48

search 40, 41, 42

shoes 48

tickle.................... 41, 42

toilet 35, 36

touch 38

touch-no 36- 38, 48

warm 39

water 44, 48

where 40, 41
.... 42, 43, 44, 48

worm 42

Verbal Language 10, 17,
.... 24, 53

Visual Acuity.................. 17

Vocal Cords 18

OTHER
SIGN with your BABY
PRODUCTS

THE VIDEO

Produced by an international-award-winning team, the *Sign with your Baby* training video is the perfect complement to the book, offering instruction, demonstration, and tips from the author, Joseph Garcia. It also features practical insight from Dr. Burton White, a leading authority on early childhood development, as well as from Speech-Language Pathologist, Alice Stroutsos, who uses signing in her practice and at home. Interviews with parents and grandparents who share their experiences, and eye-opening footage of their signing babies offer an inspirational glimpse into the power of Joseph Garcia's system.

THE QUICK REFERENCE GUIDE

This guide is designed for quick and easy visual reference to the most frequently used signs and will help you take advantage of the moments when your baby is ready to learn a new sign. This attractive illustrated index also gives you the means to monitor your baby's progress and teach other caregivers—grandparents and babysitters—the signs your baby knows. Its protective laminated covering can withstand the test of time…and an occasional splattering of applesauce.

THE COMPLETE LEARNING KIT

The Complete Learning Kit combines the *Sign with your Baby* book, video, and Quick Reference Guide to make a comprehensive educational program. The tools, instruction, and motivation provided in this powerful package will help you give your child the gift of a strong foundation to support effective communication for a lifetime.

TO ORDER

To order these and other *Sign with your Baby* products, ask your local retailer or visit our website at www.sign2me.com. To order by phone, call 206-361-0307.

NOTES:

NOTES:

NOTES: